Bowl Me Over

A Bounty of Tiny Pillows to Enjoy Every Day

Debbie Busby

Martingale
Create with Confidence

Bowl Me Over: A Bounty of Tiny Pillows to Enjoy Every Day
© 2019 by Debbie Busby

Martingale®
19021 120th Ave. NE, Ste. 102
Bothell, WA 98011-9511 USA
ShopMartingale.com

Printed in China
24 23 22 21 20 19   8 7 6 5 4 3 2 1

Library of Congress Cataloging-in-Publication Data is available upon request.

ISBN: 978-1-68356-019-7

MISSION STATEMENT

We empower makers who use fabric and yarn to make life more enjoyable.

CREDITS

**PUBLISHER AND
CHIEF VISIONARY OFFICER**
Jennifer Erbe Keltner

CONTENT DIRECTOR
Karen Costello Soltys

DESIGN MANAGER
Adrienne Smitke

MANAGING EDITOR
Tina Cook

PRODUCTION MANAGER
Regina Girard

ACQUISITIONS EDITOR
Laurie Baker

**COVER AND
BOOK DESIGNER**
Kathy Kotomaimoce

TECHNICAL EDITOR
Ellen Pahl

LOCATION PHOTOGRAPHER
Adam Albright

COPY EDITOR
Durby Peterson

STUDIO PHOTOGRAPHER
Brent Kane

ILLUSTRATOR
Sandy Loi

SPECIAL THANKS
*Photography for this book was taken at
Carol Hansen's Garden Barn in Indianola, Iowa.*

DEDICATION

In memory of my grandma, Della Jane, who sat me down next to her as a young girl with a box of fabric scraps, odds and ends of ribbons and trims, and a big bowl of colorful buttons, along with a needle and thread. Thank you, Grandma, for spending time with me and giving me so many fun memories!

Contents

What's a Bowl Filler?

When I was a child, in addition to learning to sew from my grandmothers, I learned that you should always have a bowl full of something on the coffee table. A bowl filler can be a variety of things. My memory recalls glass bowls filled with colorful hard candies— some had a soft center, which you never knew if you'd like until you got to the center, and some were beautifully striped ribbon candies that always seemed to stick together when you tried to select one. Other memories are of wooden bowls filled with assorted nuts that required cracking and shelling.

The bowl fillers in this book, however, are better for your diet! They are soft, stuffed little pillows that add a sweet touch for home and holiday decorating. They will fill your collection of cherished bowls but can also be used as pincushions, ornaments, sachets, and wreath decor. Use them in groupings or simply by themselves on a shelf or in a shallow saucer.

These little pillows feature a combination of embroidery stitches and wool appliqué on cotton or wool. The fabric and wool I've used are suggestions, and I hope you'll add your own personal touches, selecting colors and fabric to fit your home.

My bowl fillers are embellished with hand stitching, which is by far one of my favorite activities. When I learned to sew at an early age, it was with the simple tools of the trade, a needle and thread. That's when I fell in love with sewing. I soon moved on to using the sewing machine, making many articles of clothing for myself, my children, and family and friends. As years passed, I began sewing crafts for bazaars and local quilt shops, adding bits of hand stitching and embroidery here and there. It was then that I found myself coming full circle back to my first love, hand stitching.

I appreciate that hand stitching allows me to slow down a bit. I enjoy the process of making each stitch and the satisfaction that it brings. It gives me the flexibility to create almost anywhere, whether I'm by myself, waiting for an appointment, or hanging with family or a group of friends.

The projects in this book include simple motifs and hand-sewn words of encouragement using cotton fabric, pieces of wool, rickrack and trims, assorted buttons, a bag of stuffing, and naturally, a needle and thread. (And don't forget the bowl!) Of course, you'll want to sew the final pieces together by machine for strength when stuffing. I hope that these designs bring you back to the simple pleasures and joys of hand sewing.

Happy stitching!

~Debbie

Portable tools keep wool appliqué fun and friendly!

No scrap of wool is too small to save for wool appliqué.

Tools and Supplies

When I think of tools I think of my dad. He was a handyman who loved all kinds of projects and always kept his tools in tip-top shape! Having the right tools for the job is at the top of my list when beginning a project. One thing that makes wool appliqué fun and friendly is that it does not require many tools, and the tools needed are so portable.

Tools for wool appliqué and embroidery include freezer paper, a pencil, scissors, an iron, needles, appliqué pins, and threads.

Needles. Many different types and sizes of needles are available for sewing, and each is labeled for a different purpose. I find myself using embroidery and chenille needles most often, and I choose them based on the size of the eye. If I can thread it, I can stitch with it. My favorite embroidery needles are size #8. If you're using a heavier thread, a chenille #22 needle works well.

Thread. Pretty pearl cotton, embroidery floss, wool threads, and even simple quilting threads are fun to sew with. I love to use Valdani 100% cotton variegated pearl cotton, size 12. I also use a single strand of Valdani quilting thread, size 35, for a finer stitch that doesn't stand out as much. Another of my go-to favorites for years has been YLI glazed-cotton quilting thread. Whenever the materials list calls for quilting thread, that is what I've used.

The heavier the thread weight, the more it will stand out. Note that the higher the size number, the finer the thread. Use lightweight thread when stitching small areas and appliqué pieces. There is no right or wrong in choosing thread; work with what you have or what you love. If you want to use six-strand embroidery floss, two strands will look similar to size 12 pearl cotton. Use a single strand of floss for smaller appliqué pieces.

Scissors. It's important to have a pair of sharp, pointed scissors when cutting out wool pieces for appliqué. I keep an assortment of scissors on hand. One of my favorites is by Karen Kay Buckley. The blades have a serrated edge and they come in a variety of sizes. A small pair is handy when you need to cut tiny pieces and clip threads.

Cotton fabric. Appliquéing wool onto a cotton background adds dimension to these projects. When choosing a cotton background for wool appliqué and embroidery projects, woven or yarn-dyed cotton fabrics work nicely. Soft flannels and small prints are also a good choice for backgrounds for wool appliqué. Additional possibilities include tea towels, flour-sack toweling, linen, and of course, wool. Wool appliquéd onto wool is always perfect.

GIVE COTTON A BOOST

When using cotton as a background for wool appliqué, use a lightweight fusible interfacing, such as Pellon SF101 Shape-Flex Interfacing, on the wrong side for extra stability.

Wool fabric. All the wool fabric used for these projects is 100% wool that has been felted—that's my go-to choice because it gives the best outcome.

When choosing wool for appliqué, it's important to consider the weight. Wools vary from very fine, lightweight wool to flannel-weight wool to thick wool for blankets and coats. In my experience, flannel-weight wool works best. This is wool that, like cotton flannel, has a soft napped finish on one or both sides. When purchasing wool, you have a few options.

New wool or wool off the bolt. Wool that is cut off the bolt is dyed at the mill and can be found in fabric shops, quilt shops, and woolen mills. This wool can come in a variety of colors and textures and will need to be felted before use. See "Felting Wool" (at right) for directions. Look for fabric that is at least 80% wool, or it won't felt. Use 100% wool whenever possible.

Repurposed wool. You can look for wool at garage sales, estate sales, and thrift shops in the form of skirts, shirts, jackets, and lightweight blankets. It can be hard to know the fiber content of a garment if there is no tag listing it. You can experiment to see if it felts. If you don't love the color of found wool, you can overdye it.

Hand-dyed wool. Hand-dyed wool is my favorite. This wool has already been felted through the dyeing process. Hand-dyed wools can be more expensive, but they're convenient and offer many different textures and color options. They're soft and wonderful to stitch with. The depth of color adds an extra touch of richness to the projects.

Wool Appliqué

The simplicity of wool appliqué is what makes it so easy. Wool that has been felted can be cut into shapes without the edges raveling, which means there is no need to turn under the edges when appliquéing.

Felting Wool

To felt wool is quite simple. The felting process requires moisture, agitation, and heat, which cause the wool fibers to shrink and tighten, making the wool thicker and preventing the cut edges from fraying. If you're working with repurposed wool from a garment, I recommend taking the garment apart before felting it.

Sort the wool by color or by lights and darks. Using a small amount of laundry soap, set the washer for a normal wash cycle with hot water, followed by a cold rinse. The change of temperature helps in the felting process. Follow up by drying the wool on high heat. You can place a clean, dry towel in the dryer with the wool to help absorb extra moisture and cut down on drying time. Remove the wool from the dryer and lay it flat to prevent wrinkling. Felting wool can produce a lot of lint, so be sure to clean out the lint trap.

Cutting Wool Appliqués

Cutting out appliqué shapes is easy with the use of freezer paper, which you can find at most grocery stores. Some quilt shops carry freezer paper in sheets, such as *Kim Diehl's Best Appliqué Freezer Paper*. Freezer paper has a dull side and a shiny side. Always trace appliqué shapes onto the dull side with the shiny side down.

1 Place the freezer paper shiny side down over the pattern; you'll be able to see through the freezer paper well enough to trace the shape. Use a pencil or permanent marker so that ink won't rub off onto your hands or the wool. It's helpful to label the pieces as you trace them so you'll know which wool to use when you get to the ironing board. Leave at least ⅛" of space between traced patterns.

2 Cut out the freezer-paper shapes ¼" outside the traced line. *Do not cut on the traced line yet.*

3 Set the iron to the wool setting and turn on the steam. With the shiny side down, iron each freezer-paper shape onto the appropriate color of wool. If you're cutting multiple pieces from the same piece of wool, place the shapes close together to maximize the use of the wool.

4 Cut out the appliqué piece on the traced line, cutting through the freezer paper and wool at the same time.

5 Remove the freezer paper from the wool before you appliqué. If you have multiple pieces that are similar in shape and size, it's helpful to keep the labeled freezer paper on them until you have positioned everything on the background fabric.

6 Place the background on a flat surface and position the appliqué pieces on it. Pin the pieces in place with appliqué pins, which are short and less likely to catch the thread. My favorites are Clover appliqué pins. To make sure that everything is in its proper place, it works best to position all the appliqué pieces on the background for placement before beginning stitching. Then remove the topmost pieces and stitch the bottom layer of appliqués first.

TIPS FOR TINY PIECES

Some of the pieces are small, and pulling too hard can distort the appliqués, so it's important to handle the small appliqué pieces gently. Use a dab of Dritz Fray Check (a liquid sealant) to keep tiny pieces from fraying.

7 Stitch around the edge of each appliqué to secure it to the background. I use the blanket stitch or the whipstitch. The blanket stitch takes a bit more time and thread but gives a great look and outlines the design. The whipstitch is quick and easy and uses less thread. I usually whipstitch small appliqué pieces, as it gives a less bulky look. See the "Stitch Guide" (page 10) if you're unfamiliar with these stitches.

8 When the appliqué is complete, press the project to give it a fresh look. Using steam, press from the back first. Turn the piece over and use a pressing cloth (I use a scrap of light-colored cotton) on the front to prevent overheating or scorching the wool pieces.

Embroidery

Here you'll find techniques for transferring embroidery designs to fabric, along with a guide to the embroidery stitches used throughout the book. When transferring embroidery designs onto the fabric, you'll use different methods depending on the weight and color of the fabric. If you're unsure how to get the designs onto the fabric for easy stitching, read on.

Light-Colored Cotton

You can easily trace the design onto light-colored cotton fabric with the help of a light box or window.

1 Lay the embroidery pattern on the light box or secure it to the window with painter's tape.

2 Position and tape the fabric over the pattern. Trace the design very lightly with a pencil, water-soluble marker, or a Pilot FriXion pen (my preference), which disappears with the heat of an iron.

Dark Cotton or Wool

When transferring an embroidery design onto a dark cotton or heavier fabric such as wool, I recommend Glad Press'n Seal, which is available at most grocery stores with the plastic wraps and wax paper. The product has a smooth side and a tacky side. Always use it with the tacky side down. It's important to use a *permanent* fine-point marker to trace the designs so that the ink won't smear or rub off onto your hands or project. If the wool is very dark, it's helpful to use a *colored* permanent marker, such as silver or bright pink, rather than black. The design will show up better when the Press'n Seal is placed on the dark fabric.

1 Cut a piece of Press'n Seal large enough to cover the embroidery design or appliqué shape. With the tacky side down, carefully lay the Press'n Seal over the pattern and smooth out any wrinkles. Use a permanent marker to trace the pattern directly onto the smooth side of the plastic wrap.

2 After the ink has dried, lift the marked Press'n Seal and position it on the fabric, pressing it and smoothing out any wrinkles with your hands. The plastic wrap will stay in place on its own. Trim away any excess that extends beyond the edges of the fabric.

3 Embroider the designs, stitching through the Press'n Seal. For best results, make the stitches a bit more taut than you normally would because removing the plastic will exert tension on the

stitching. If the pattern includes lazy daisy stitches, it's best to wait until you've removed the Press'n Seal to make them. Because lazy daisy stitches are a bit loose, it's easy to distort them as you remove the plastic wrap.

4 When you've finished the embroidery, carefully peel away the Press'n Seal from the fabric and stitches. Use a small pair of tweezers to remove any bits of plastic wrap that are difficult to detach.

Stitch Guide

Below are the stitches used throughout the book. I don't use an embroidery hoop when stitching these bowl fillers.

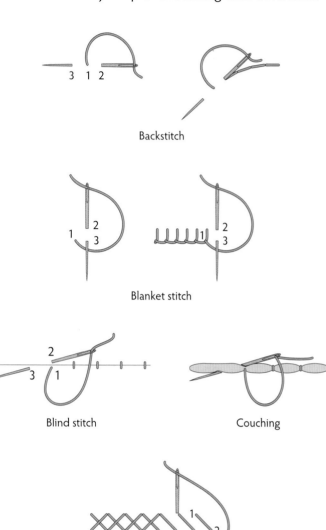

Backstitch

Blanket stitch

Blind stitch   Couching

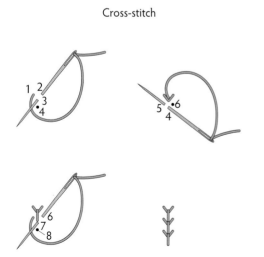

Cross-stitch

Fly stitch

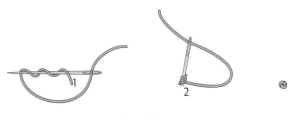

French knot

Lazy daisy

Running stitch   Satin stitch

Stem stitch

Straight stitch

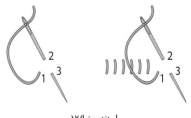

Whipstitch

When sewing the front and back of the bowl filler pillow together, you have a choice of two methods for creating an opening for stuffing, as follows.

Leaving an Opening

1 Place the front and back of the pillow right sides together, centering the front on the back. (The back will be larger than the front, but it will be trimmed even after stitching.) The pillow front should be wrong side up.

2 Using a ¼" seam allowance, sew around the edge of the pillow front and leave an opening along the bottom that's approximately 1½" to 2", depending on the size of the pillow.

¼"

3 Trim the excess fabric to make all the seam allowances even. Trim the corners of rectangles and squares. Clip the curves of round shapes.

4 Turn the pillow right side out through the opening and stuff lightly. Blindstitch the opening closed.

Cutting a Slit

1 Follow steps 1–3 of "Leaving an Opening" beginning on page 11, but sew all the way around; do not leave an opening.

2 Carefully cut an opening, approximately 1½" to 2" long, in the back of the pillow. Be careful to cut *only* through the back layer!

3 Turn the pillow right side out, stuff it lightly, and whipstitch the opening closed. My favorite stuffing tool is a hemostat, which is helpful for grabbing and pushing small bits of stuffing into a pillow right where you need it.

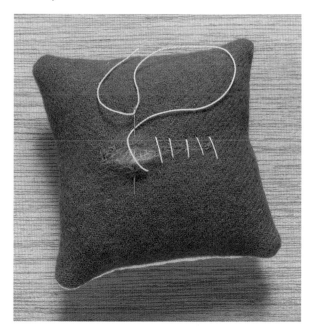

4 Cut a rectangular scrap of wool large enough to cover the slit; whipstitch it over the top of the opening. For added fun, I sometimes embroider a word on the rectangle of wool before stitching it to the pillow back.

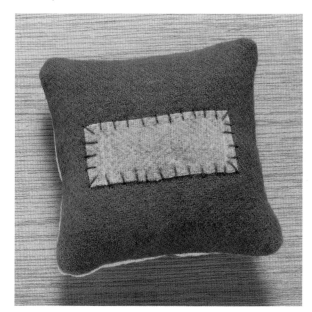

our home

We love having guests in our home. Stitching some sweet and simple
words, phrases, and hearts to scatter around or add to a bowl in the guest
room will make your guests feel loved and welcome for sure!

Welcome

Materials

- 3" × 6½" rectangle of cream cotton for front*
- 1¾" × 6½" rectangle of blue cotton print for front
- 4¼" × 6½" rectangle of brown wool for back
- 1½" × 1½" square of burgundy wool for heart
- 2 rectangles, 4¼" × 6½", of lightweight fusible interfacing
- Brown pearl cotton, size 12
- Burgundy Rustic Wool Moire thread**
- Fiberfill stuffing

*The bowl filler shown is made from On Point cotton by Maywood Studio.

**See "Resources" (page 80) for additional information.

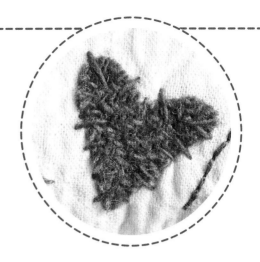

Stitching and Assembly

Press the seam allowances as shown by the arrow.

1. Sew the cream 3" × 6½" rectangle and blue 1¾" × 6½" rectangle together to create the front, which should measure 4¼" × 6½", including seam allowances.

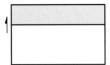

Make 1 unit,
4¼" × 6½".

2. Fuse the interfacing to the wrong sides of the front and back pieces, following the manufacturer's instructions.

3. Transfer the letters from the pattern below onto the cream cotton section of the front.

4. Backstitch the letters *W, e, l, c, m,* and *e* using brown pearl cotton.

5. Use the heart pattern to cut the appliqué from the burgundy wool and whipstitch it in place using the wool thread.

6. Trim the stitched piece to 5½" × 3¼".

7. Referring to "Assembling the Bowl Fillers" (page 11), sew and stuff the pillow.

Appliqué pattern does not
include seam allowances.

Heart
Cut 1
burgundy.

Welcome Bowl Filler

Embroidery Key

- - - - - Backstitch

Filled with Love

Materials

- ✕ 5½" × 11" rectangle of red cotton print for heart
- ✕ 1¼" × 2" rectangle of blue wool for appliquéd patch
- ✕ 5½" × 11" rectangle of lightweight fusible interfacing
- ✕ Light brown cotton quilting thread
- ✕ 1 white button, ¾" diameter
- ✕ 1 brown button, ⅜" diameter
- ✕ 1 white button, ½" diameter
- ✕ Template plastic or cardstock
- ✕ Fiberfill stuffing

Stitching and Assembly

1 Fuse the interfacing to the wrong side of the red rectangle, following the manufacturer's instructions.

2 Cut the rectangle into two squares that measure 5½" × 5½".

3 Make a template using the heart pattern below and trace it onto the wrong side of one of the red squares. Do not cut out the heart.

4 Place the red squares right sides together, with raw edges aligned. Pin at the corners to secure the fabric and then sew on the traced line completely around the heart.

5 Trim around the heart, leaving a ¼" seam allowance. Clip into the deep inner point at the top of the heart. Carefully cut a 1½" slit in the fabric on one side of the heart to make an opening for turning and stuffing.

6 Turn and stuff the heart lightly; whipstitch the opening closed.

7 Place the blue wool rectangle over the stitched opening and whipstitch it with light brown thread.

8 Stack and sew the larger white button and the brown button on top of the patch, sewing through the center of the heart and out the back using brown thread. Add the ½" white button to the other side. Sew back and forth several times from front to back through all the buttons, pulling the thread taut as you stitch. Knot the thread and bury the knot in the stuffing.

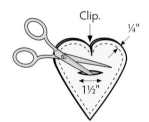

Clip.

¼"

1½"

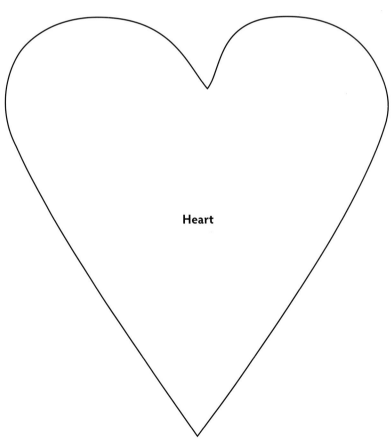

Heart

Filled with Love Bowl Filler

Memories of Grandma's House

Materials

- × 5" × 5½" rectangle of brown cotton print for front
- × 5" × 5½" rectangle of brown wool for back
- × 2 rectangles, 5" × 5½", of lightweight fusible interfacing
- × 3½" × 4" cotton lace heart doily*
- × Cream pearl cotton, size 12
- × Brown cotton quilting thread
- × 7 assorted buttons
- × Fiberfill stuffing

*Size is approximate. See "Resources" (page 80).

Stitching and Assembly

1 Fuse the interfacing to the wrong sides of the brown print and brown wool rectangles, following the manufacturer's instructions.

2 Center and pin the doily on the brown cotton. Sew the doily to the front using cream pearl cotton and a blanket stitch around the outer edge. Feel free to add extra stitching in and around the doily as desired. I added running stitches inside the heart and a French knot at the bottom using burgundy wool thread.

3 Trim the stitched piece to 4½" × 5".

4 Referring to "Assembling the Bowl Fillers" (page 11), sew and stuff the pillow.

5 Sew the assorted buttons randomly on the doily using brown thread.

blackboard blessed

Do you remember being called to the blackboard to write spelling words or an arithmetic problem? It was even better being chosen to go outside and bang the chalk dust off the erasers on the brick wall of the school building!

Blessed

FINISHED SIZE
6½" × 2¾"

Materials

- ✗ 4" × 6½" rectangle of black cotton for front
- ✗ 2" × 4" rectangle of black-and-white plaid cotton for front
- ✗ 4" × 8" rectangle of black-and-white plaid cotton for back
- ✗ 2 rectangles, 4" × 8", of lightweight fusible interfacing
- ✗ White quilting thread
- ✗ White Uni-ball Signo Broad gel pen
- ✗ Fiberfill stuffing
- ✗ White chalk

Stitching and Assembly

Press the seam allowances as shown by the arrow.

1 Sew the plaid 2" × 4" rectangle to the black 4" × 6½" rectangle to create the front, which should measure 4" × 8", including seam allowances.

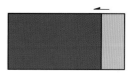

Make 1 unit,
4" × 8".

2 Fuse the interfacing to the wrong sides of the front and back pieces, following the manufacturer's instructions.

3 Transfer all embroidery lines and letters from the pattern below onto the black cotton section of the front.

4 Backstitch the word *blessed* and the scroll using white thread.

5 Color the open spaces of the word *blessed* and the scroll with the gel pen and let dry.

6 Trim the stitched piece to 7" × 3¼".

7 Referring to "Assembling the Bowl Fillers" (page 11), sew and stuff the pillow.

8 Rub the side of a piece of white chalk back and forth over the bowl filler front to give it a chalkboard look.

CHALK IT UP!

When choosing black fabric for these bowl fillers, look for one with texture, such as a woven or yarn-dyed cotton. Marcus Fabrics has a line called Basecloth that works great for a chalkboard background.

Use a white Uni-ball Signo Broad gel pen to fill in the letters and shapes on these chalkboard bowl fillers.

Rub the side of a piece of white chalk over the completed project to give it the look of a blackboard from your school days.

Embroidery Key

- - - - - Backstitch

Blessed Bowl Filler

Hope

FINISHED SIZE
5½" × 4½"

Materials

× 6" × 7" rectangle of black cotton for front

× 6" × 7" rectangle of gray cotton for back

× 2 rectangles, 6" × 7", of lightweight fusible interfacing

× White pearl cotton, size 12

× White quilting thread

× White Uni-ball Signo Broad gel pen

× Fiberfill stuffing

× White chalk

Stitching and Assembly

1 Fuse the interfacing to the wrong sides of the front and back pieces, following the manufacturer's instructions.

2 Transfer all embroidery lines and letters from the pattern below onto the black cotton.

3 Backstitch the word *Hope* using white pearl cotton.

4 Stem-stitch the outer borderline using white pearl cotton.

5 Backstitch the inner borderline using white quilting thread.

6 Make French knots using white pearl cotton.

7 Color the open spaces of the word *Hope* with the gel pen and let dry.

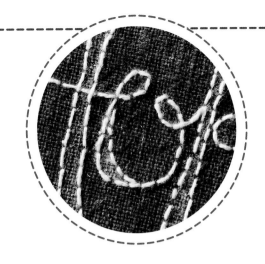

8 Trim the piece to 6" × 5", keeping the design centered.

9 Referring to "Assembling the Bowl Fillers" (page 11), sew and stuff the pillow.

10 Rub the side of a piece of white chalk back and forth over the bowl filler front to give it a chalkboard look.

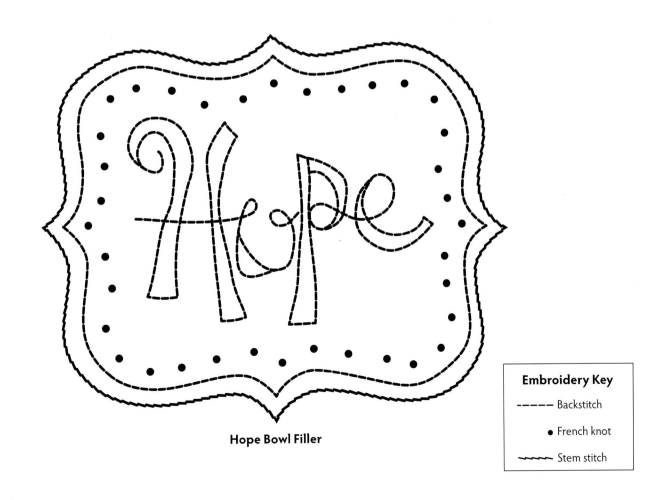

Hope Bowl Filler

Embroidery Key

- - - - - Backstitch

• French knot

⌁⌁⌁ Stem stitch

Hello

FINISHED SIZE
6½" × 4½"

Materials

- × 6" × 8" rectangle of black cotton for front
- × 6" × 8" rectangle of black-and-white plaid cotton for back
- × 2 rectangles, 6" × 8", of lightweight fusible interfacing
- × White pearl cotton, size 12
- × White Uni-ball Signo Broad gel pen
- × Fiberfill stuffing
- × White chalk

Stitching and Assembly

1 Fuse the interfacing to the wrong sides of the front and back pieces, following the manufacturer's instructions.

2 Transfer all embroidery lines and letters from the pattern below onto the black cotton.

3 Backstitch the word *hello,* the vine, and the leaves using white pearl cotton.

4 Color the open spaces of the word *hello* and the leaves with the gel pen and let dry.

5 Trim the stitched piece to 7" × 5", keeping the design centered.

6 Referring to "Assembling the Bowl Fillers" (page 11), sew and stuff the pillow.

7 Rub the side of a piece of white chalk back and forth over the bowl filler front to give it a chalkboard look.

Hello Bowl Filler

Embroidery Key
- - - - - Backstitch

Smile

FINISHED SIZE
5½" × 4"

Materials

- × 5½" × 7" rectangle of black cotton for front
- × 5½" × 7" rectangle of black-and-white striped cotton for back
- × 2 rectangles, 5½" × 7", of lightweight fusible interfacing
- × White quilting thread
- × White Uni-ball Signo Broad gel pen
- × Fiberfill stuffing
- × White chalk

Stitching and Assembly

1 Fuse the interfacing to the wrong sides of the front and back pieces, following the manufacturer's instructions.

2 Transfer all embroidery lines and letters from the pattern below onto the black cotton.

3 Using white thread, backstitch the word *Smile* and add a French knot and five lazy daisy stitches above the *i*.

4 Color the open spaces of the word *Smile* and around the lazy daisy stitches with the gel pen and let dry.

5 Trim the stitched piece to 6" × 4½".

6 Referring to "Assembling the Bowl Fillers" (page 11), sew and stuff the pillow.

7 Rub the side of a piece of white chalk back and forth over the bowl filler front to give it a chalkboard look.

Smile Bowl Filler

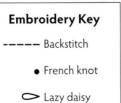

Embroidery Key

‑ ‑ ‑ ‑ ‑ Backstitch

● French knot

⌒ Lazy daisy

into the woods

My love for the forest and evergreen trees came from growing up
in the Pacific Northwest. These charming woodsy bowl fillers
are so sweet tucked into a basket or bowl with a few pinecones.

Welcome to Our Neck of the Woods

Materials

- ✕ 6" × 8" rectangle of muslin for front
- ✕ 6" × 8" rectangle of dark brown wool for back
- ✕ 2" × 2½" rectangle of dark green wool for tree
- ✕ 2" × 2½" rectangle of light green wool for tree
- ✕ 1½" × 2" rectangle of brown wool for tree trunks
- ✕ 2 rectangles, 6" × 8", of lightweight fusible interfacing
- ✕ Pearl cotton, size 12, in black, brown, and green
- ✕ Fiberfill stuffing

Stitching and Assembly

1 Fuse the interfacing to the wrong sides of the front and back pieces, following the manufacturer's instructions.

2 Use the patterns below to cut the appliqué pieces for the trees and trunks from the wool as directed.

3 Transfer the embroidery letters onto the muslin and backstitch them with black pearl cotton.

4 Position and pin the appliqué pieces on the muslin, referring to the photo on page 29 and the pattern below for placement.

5 Whipstitch around the appliqué pieces with coordinating pearl cotton.

6 Trim the stitched piece to 6½" × 5", keeping the design centered.

7 Referring to "Assembling the Bowl Fillers" (page 11), sew and stuff the pillow.

Appliqué patterns do not include seam allowances.

WELCOME TO OUR NECK OF THE WOODS

Tree 1
Cut 1 dark green.

Tree 2
Cut 1 light green.

Tree trunks
Cut 1 of each brown.

Welcome to Our Neck of the Woods Bowl Filler

Embroidery Key

- - - - - Backstitch

Tall Forest Tree

FINISHED SIZE
4" × 7¾"

Materials

- ✗ 5½" × 9½" rectangle of muslin for front
- ✗ 5½" × 9½" rectangle of brown wool for back
- ✗ 4" × 5" rectangle of green wool for tree
- ✗ 1" × 3½" rectangle of brown wool for tree trunk
- ✗ 2 rectangles, 5½" × 9½", of lightweight fusible interfacing
- ✗ Pearl cotton, size 12, in green, brown, and black
- ✗ Fiberfill stuffing

Stitching and Assembly

1 Fuse the interfacing to the wrong sides of the muslin and brown wool 5½" × 9½" rectangles, following the manufacturer's instructions.

2 Use the patterns (page 32) to cut the tree from green wool and tree trunk from brown wool.

3 Position and pin the appliqué pieces on the muslin. Blanket-stitch with coordinating pearl cotton.

<u>4</u> Embellish the tree by making straight stitches with couching in green pearl cotton. Make cross-stitches on the tree trunk with brown pearl cotton.

<u>5</u> Transfer the word *forest* next to the tree trunk using the dotted line as a placement guide. Embroider using a backstitch and black pearl cotton.

<u>6</u> Trim the stitched piece to 4½" × 8¼", keeping the design centered.

<u>7</u> Referring to "Assembling the Bowl Fillers" (page 11), sew and stuff the pillow.

Appliqué patterns do not include seam allowances.

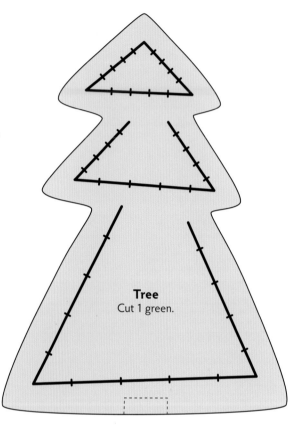

Tree
Cut 1 green.

Align with right edge of tree trunk.

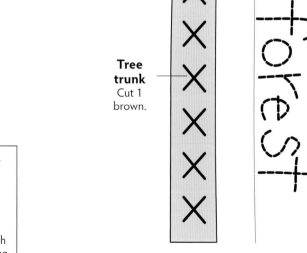

Tree trunk
Cut 1 brown.

Tall Forest Tree Bowl Filler

Embroidery Key

- - - - - Backstitch

✗ Cross-stitch

+—+—+ Straight stitch with couching

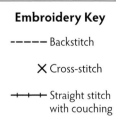

Two Short Trees

FINISHED SIZE
3½" × 6"

Materials for Both Bowl Fillers

- ✕ 2 rectangles, 5" × 7½", of muslin for fronts
- ✕ 2 rectangles, 5" × 7½", of green wool for backs
- ✕ 2 rectangles, 3½" × 4", of green wool for trees
- ✕ 2 rectangles, 1" × 3", of brown wool for tree trunks
- ✕ 4 rectangles, 5" × 7½", of lightweight fusible interfacing
- ✕ Pearl cotton, size 12, in green, brown, and black
- ✕ Fiberfill stuffing

Stitching and Assembly

1 Fuse the interfacing to the wrong sides of the muslin and green wool 5" × 7½" rectangles, following the manufacturer's instructions.

2 Use the patterns (page 34) to cut the trees and tree trunks from the wool as directed.

3 Position and pin one tree and one trunk on a muslin rectangle for each pillow. Blanket-stitch with coordinating pearl cotton.

4 Sew embellishing stitches on the trees with green pearl cotton. I made straight stitches with couching on the *Tree* version. On the *Woods* version, I added backstitching next to the blanket stitching. Sew cross-stitches in the center of the tree trunks with brown pearl cotton.

5 Transfer the word *Tree* or *Woods* next to the tree trunk using the dotted lines as placement guides. Embroider using a backstitch and black pearl cotton.

6 Trim the stitched pieces to 4" × 6½", keeping the designs centered.

7 Referring to "Assembling the Bowl Fillers" (page 11), sew and stuff the pillows.

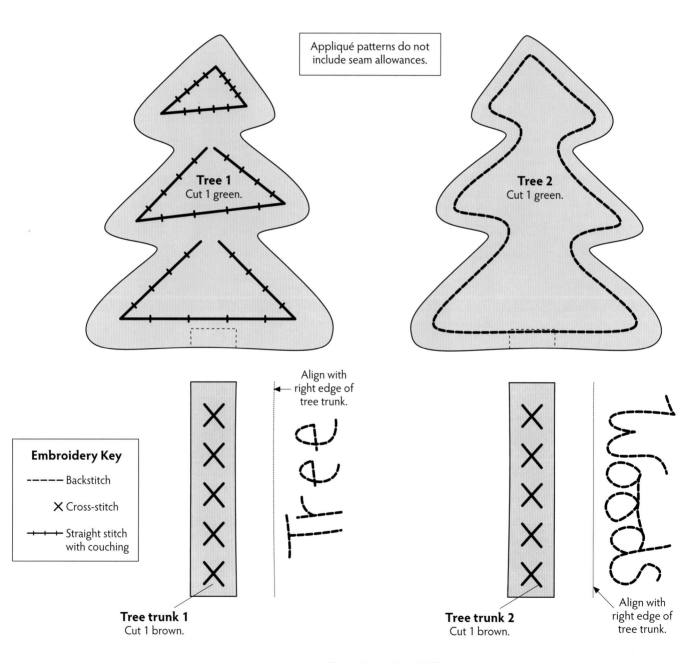

Appliqué patterns do not include seam allowances.

Tree 1
Cut 1 green.

Tree 2
Cut 1 green.

Align with right edge of tree trunk.

Embroidery Key

----- Backstitch

✕ Cross-stitch

+—+—+ Straight stitch with couching

Tree trunk 1
Cut 1 brown.

Tree trunk 2
Cut 1 brown.

Align with right edge of tree trunk.

Two Short Trees Bowl Fillers

Our Cabin

Materials

- ✕ 4½" × 7" rectangle of muslin for front
- ✕ 4½" × 7" rectangle of dark cotton for back
- ✕ 2 rectangles, 4½" × 7", of lightweight fusible interfacing
- ✕ Pearl cotton, size 12, in black, brown, and green
- ✕ 3 brown buttons, ⅜" diameter
- ✕ Fiberfill stuffing

Stitching and Assembly

1 Fuse the interfacing to the wrong sides of the muslin and dark cotton rectangles, following the manufacturer's instructions.

2 Transfer the words *our cabin* and the embroidery design from the pattern below onto the center of the muslin.

3 Backstitch the words using black pearl cotton and the branch using brown pearl cotton. Stitch the pine needles with a straight stitch and green pearl cotton.

4 Trim the stitched piece to 6" × 3½", keeping the design centered.

5 Sew the three buttons in place.

6 Referring to "Assembling the Bowl Fillers" (page 11), sew and stuff the pillow.

Button
placement

Our Cabin Bowl Filler

Embroidery Key
----- Backstitch
—— Straight stitch

making a house a home

Welcome home! That's just how this collection of bowl fillers will make you feel—welcomed. Displaying an arrangement of these sweet, homey pillows will warm up any room, because each one is lovingly stitched with friendly words and motifs.

Happy Home

THIS IS OUR HAPPY PLACE

FINISHED SIZE
4¼" × 5"

Materials

- × 6" × 6½" rectangle of cream cotton for front*
- × 6" × 6½" rectangle of dark cotton for back
- × 2 rectangles, ½" × 3¾", of blue wool for top and bottom trim
- × 2 rectangles, 6" × 6½", of lightweight fusible interfacing
- × Pearl cotton, size 12, in blue, mauve, and brown variegated
- × 1 brown button, ½" diameter
- × Fiberfill stuffing

*The bowl filler shown is made from Diamond Textiles Primitive Collection.

1 Fuse the interfacing to the wrong sides of the cream and dark cotton rectangles, following the manufacturer's instructions.

2 Transfer the words *This is our Happy Place* from the pattern (page 40) onto the cream cotton.

3 Using the brown variegated pearl cotton, backstitch the words and add a French knot above each *i*.

4 Pin the blue wool rectangles in place and whipstitch them with blue pearl cotton.

5 Add cross-stitches to the blue wool with mauve pearl cotton.

6 Sew the button in place.

7 Trim the stitched piece to 4¾" × 5½".

8 Referring to "Assembling the Bowl Fillers" (page 11), sew and stuff the pillow.

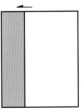

You + Me = Home

Press the seam allowances as shown by the arrow.

1 Sew the light brown 2" × 6½" rectangle to the light 4" × 6½" rectangle to create the front, which should measure 5½" × 6½", including seam allowances.

Make 1 unit,
5½" × 6½".

2 Fuse the interfacing to the wrong sides of the front and back pieces, following the manufacturer's instructions.

3 Transfer all of the embroidery letters from the pattern (page 40) onto the light section of the front piece.

4 Backstitch the words *you + me = home* using brown pearl cotton.

5 Sew the five cream buttons in place on the brown print as shown on the pattern.

6 Trim the piece to 4¼" × 5½".

7 Referring to "Assembling the Bowl Fillers" (page 11), sew and stuff the pillow.

FINISHED SIZE
3¾" × 5"

Materials

× 2" × 6½" rectangle of light brown cotton print for front

× 4" × 6½" rectangle of light cotton for front*

× 5½" × 6½" rectangle of dark brown cotton for back

× 2 rectangles, 5½" × 6½", of lightweight fusible interfacing

× Brown pearl cotton, size 12

× 5 cream buttons, ½" diameter

× Fiberfill stuffing

The bowl filler shown is made from On Point cotton by Maywood Studio.

Align with seam.

Button placement

Embroidery Key

----- Backstitch

You + Me = Home Bowl Filler

Appliqué placement

Button placement

Embroidery Key

----- Backstitch

✕ Cross-stitch

• French knot

This Is Our Happy Place Bowl Filler

Stay Awhile

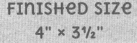

Materials

- ✕ 6" × 6" square of cream cotton for front*
- ✕ 6" × 6" square of blue wool for back
- ✕ 2 squares, 6" × 6", of lightweight fusible interfacing
- ✕ Pearl cotton, size 12, in brown and dark brown
- ✕ Burgundy Rustic Wool Moire thread**
- ✕ Fiberfill stuffing

*The bowl filler shown is made of On Point cotton (Natural) by Maywood Studio.

**Debbie used color #282. See "Resources" (page 80) for where to purchase.

Stitching and Assembly

1 Fuse the interfacing to the wrong sides of the cream cotton and blue wool squares, following the manufacturer's instructions.

2 Transfer all embroidery lines and letters from the pattern (page 42) onto the cream cotton. Also trace the outer hexagon, which will be the cutting line after stitching.

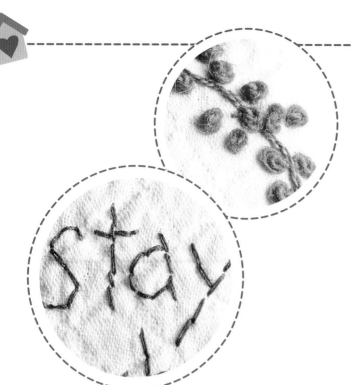

3. Stitch the wreath vine with a stem stitch using brown pearl cotton.

4. Backstitch the words *Stay Awhile* using dark brown pearl cotton. Stitch a French knot above the *i*.

5. Stitch French knots around the inside and outside of the wreath vine with burgundy wool thread.

6. Trim the stitched piece using the outer traced line to create a hexagon shape.

7. Referring to "Assembling the Bowl Fillers" (page 11), sew and stuff the pillow.

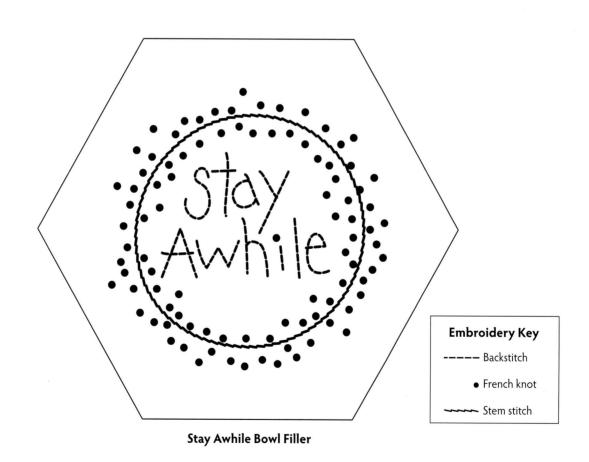

Stay Awhile Bowl Filler

Embroidery Key

- - - - - Backstitch

• French knot

∿∿∿ Stem stitch

Rest Easy

THere'S NO PLACe LIKe HOme

FINISHeD SIZe
4¼" × 6⅛"

Materials

- ✗ 6" × 7½" rectangle of brown cotton for front
- ✗ 6" × 7½" rectangle of cream cotton for back
- ✗ 4" × 6" rectangle of blue wool for house
- ✗ 3" × 5" rectangle of dark brown wool for roof
- ✗ 1" × 2" rectangle of burgundy wool for door
- ✗ 2 rectangles, 6" × 7½", of lightweight fusible interfacing
- ✗ Pearl cotton, size 12, in blue, gray variegated, burgundy, and light brown variegated
- ✗ Fiberfill stuffing
- ✗ Small key or other charm

1 Fuse the interfacing to the wrong sides of the cream and brown cotton rectangles, following the manufacturer's instructions.

2 Use the patterns (page 45) to cut out the house, roof, and door appliqués.

3 Position and pin the house and roof onto the brown cotton. Blanket-stitch around the house and roof using coordinating pearl cotton.

4 Position the door and whipstitch using burgundy pearl cotton.

5 Transfer the words *There's no place like HOME* from the pattern onto the house and backstitch them using gray variegated pearl cotton.

6 Using light brown variegated pearl cotton, make a line of fly stitches on each side of the roof and add a French knot at the peak of the roof.

7 Trim the stitched front ½" from the appliquéd house and roof to create the house shape.

8 Referring to "Assembling the Bowl Fillers" (page 11), sew and stuff the pillow.

9 Hand sew the key charm to the bowl filler.

Be our Guest

Press the seam allowances as shown by the arrows.

1 Cut the brown print into four strips, 1¼" × 7".

2 Sew a border strip to each side of the cream 2½" × 5¼" rectangle, beginning along the top and working clockwise around the center. Trim the excess border fabric even with the center after sewing each side to create the front, which should measure 4" × 6¾", including seam allowances.

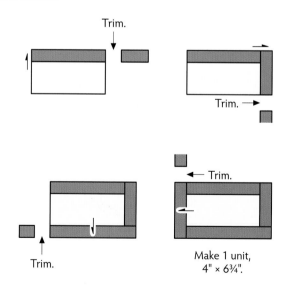

Trim.

Trim.

Trim.

Trim.

Make 1 unit, 4" × 6¾".

FINISHED SIZE
6" × 3¼"

Materials

× 6" × 7" rectangle of brown print cotton for front border

× 2½" × 5¼" rectangle of cream cotton for front*

× 4" × 6¾" rectangle of cream cotton for back

× 2 rectangles, 4" × 6¾", of lightweight fusible interfacing

× Brown variegated pearl cotton, size 12

× Fiberfill stuffing

× 5 or 6 white or cream buttons

The bowl filler shown is made from Daiwabo Taupe Woven.

3 Fuse the interfacing to the wrong sides of the pieced front and the 4" × 6¾" cream rectangle, following the manufacturer's instructions.

4 Transfer the words *be our guest* from the pattern below onto the cream section of the front.

5 Backstitch the words using brown variegated pearl cotton.

6 Trim the stitched piece to 6½" × 3¾".

7 Referring to "Assembling the Bowl Fillers" (page 11), sew and stuff the pillow.

8 Thread the buttons onto a length of pearl cotton and pin or stitch them to the bowl filler.

Appliqué patterns do not include seam allowances.

Embroidery Key

----- Backstitch

∨ Fly stitch

● French knot

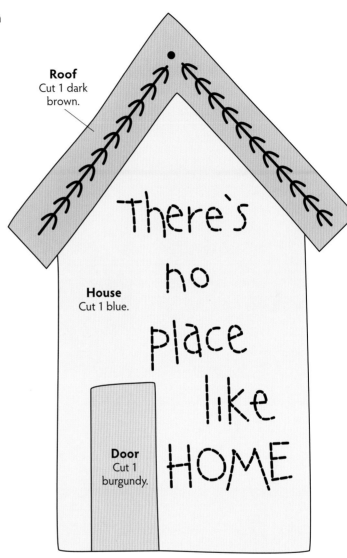

There's No Place Like Home Bowl Filler

Be Our Guest Bowl Filler

Embroidery Key

----- Backstitch

Home Is Where the Heart Is

FINISHED SIZE
6" × 3¼"

Materials

- ✕ 5" × 7½" rectangle of cream cotton for front*
- ✕ 5" × 7½" rectangle of dark cotton for back
- ✕ 2½" × 4½" rectangle of brown wool for letters
- ✕ 2" × 2½" rectangle of blue wool for house
- ✕ 1½" × 2¼" rectangle of dark brown wool for roof
- ✕ 1½" × 1½" square of burgundy wool for heart
- ✕ 2 rectangles, 5" × 7½", of lightweight fusible interfacing
- ✕ Brown quilting thread
- ✕ Pearl cotton, size 12, in blue, dark brown, and burgundy
- ✕ Fiberfill stuffing

The bowl filler shown is made from Daiwabo Taupe Woven.

Stitching and Assembly

1 Fuse the interfacing to the wrong sides of the cream and dark cotton rectangles, following the manufacturer's instructions.

2 Use the pattern below to cut out the letters *H, M,* and *E* from the brown wool. Cut the house from the blue wool, the roof from the dark brown wool, and the heart from the burgundy wool.

3 Position and pin the letters, house, roof, and heart on the cream cotton. Whipstitch the letters with brown thread. Whipstitch the house, roof, and heart with coordinating pearl cotton.

4 Transfer the words *is where the heart is* from the pattern and backstitch with brown quilting thread. Stitch a French knot above each *i.*

5 Trim the stitched piece to 6½" × 3¾", keeping the design centered.

6 Referring to "Assembling the Bowl Fillers" (page 11), sew and stuff the pillow.

THINGS TO FILL

Putting bowl fillers into a bowl is just the beginning of what you can do with them. Also try filling shallow baskets, wire baskets, pie plates, wooden bowls, old ironstone plates, or vintage dishes. Whatever you choose, the key is to look for a somewhat shallow vessel. Garage sales or thrift shops can be fun places to hunt for these items.

You can complement the bowl fillers with a base of fun little objects such as old buttons, pebbles, potpourri, old wooden spools, glass beads, coffee beans, and popcorn kernels. I'm sure you can think of even more ideas for backfill!

Appliqué patterns do not include seam allowances.

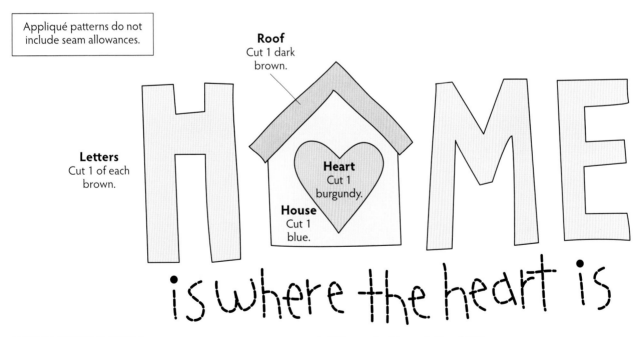

Roof
Cut 1 dark brown.

Letters
Cut 1 of each brown.

Heart
Cut 1 burgundy.

House
Cut 1 blue.

Home Is Where the Heart Is Bowl Filler

Embroidery Key

- - - - - Backstitch

● French knot

Home Sweet Home

FINISHED SIZE
4½" × 3½"

Materials

- × 5" × 6" rectangle of light brown cotton for front*
- × 5" × 6" rectangle of blue cotton print for back
- × 3" × 5" rectangle of blue wool for letters
- × 2 rectangles, 5" × 6", of lightweight fusible interfacing
- × Light brown cotton quilting thread
- × Dark brown pearl cotton, size 12
- × Fiberfill stuffing

*The bowl filler shown is made from Diamond Textiles Woven Fabric.

Stitching and Assembly

Photo on page 46.

1 Fuse the interfacing to the wrong sides of the light brown and blue cotton rectangles, following the manufacturer's instructions.

2 Use the pattern below to cut out two sets of letters for the word *HOME* from the blue wool.

3 Position the letters on the light brown rectangle using the pattern as a guide. Whipstitch the letters with light brown quilting thread.

4 Transfer the word *sweet* from the pattern and backstitch with dark brown pearl cotton.

5 Trim the stitched piece to 5" × 4", keeping the design centered.

6 Referring to "Assembling the Bowl Fillers" (page 11), sew and stuff the pillow.

Letters
Cut 1 of each blue.

HOME sweet HOME

Appliqué patterns do not include seam allowances.

Embroidery Key

----- Backstitch

Home Sweet Home Bowl Filler

bee attitudes

*As sweet as honey, these bowl fillers will lift your spirit and
encourage a positive attitude as you stitch away!*

Be Kind

FINISHED SIZE
5" × 5"

Materials

- ✕ 6½" × 6½" square of cream wool for front
- ✕ 6½" × 6½" square of cream polka-dot cotton for back
- ✕ 5" × 5" square of black wool for scalloped border and bee head
- ✕ 2" × 2" square of gold wool for bee body
- ✕ 1½" × 3" rectangle of beige wool for bee wings
- ✕ 2 squares, 6½" × 6½", of lightweight fusible interfacing
- ✕ Pearl cotton, size 12, in black, cream, green, white, and gold
- ✕ Black cotton quilting thread
- ✕ Fiberfill stuffing

Stitching and Assembly

1 Fuse the interfacing to the wrong sides of the cream wool and cream polka-dot squares, following the manufacturer's instructions.

2 Use the patterns (page 51) to cut the scalloped border and bee head from the black wool. Cut the bee body from the gold wool and the bee wings from the beige wool.

3 Position and pin the appliqué pieces on the cream wool square. Use coordinating pearl cotton to whipstitch the scalloped border, bee head, and bee wings.

4 Blanket-stitch the bee body with coordinating pearl cotton. Use black pearl cotton to sew straight stitches across the body for stripes. Add couching stitches to hold the thread in place.

5 Use white pearl cotton to sew straight stitches on the wings as shown in the photo on page 50. Add couching stitches to hold the thread in place.

6 Backstitch the bee antennae with black pearl cotton and sew a French knot at the top of each.

7 Use green pearl cotton to sew a cross-stitch in each scallop of the border (four cross-stitches per side).

8 Use the pattern to transfer the words *bee kind* and backstitch them using black thread.

9 Trim the stitched piece to 5½" square.

10 Referring to "Assembling the Bowl Fillers" (page 11), sew and stuff the pillow.

Appliqué patterns do not include seam allowances.

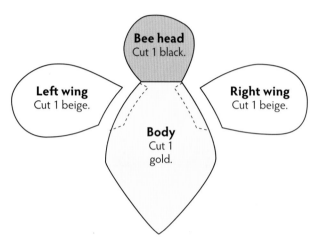

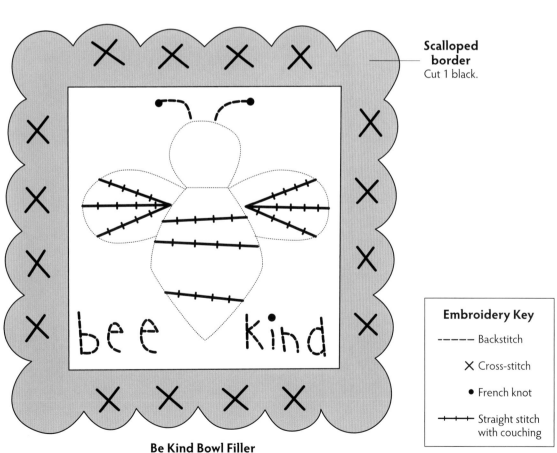

Be Kind Bowl Filler

Embroidery Key

----- Backstitch

✕ Cross-stitch

● French knot

+++++ Straight stitch with couching

Be Happy

FINISHED SIZE
3½" × 3½"

Materials

- ✕ 5" × 5" square of cream cotton for front*
- ✕ 5" × 5" square of gold wool for back
- ✕ 3½" × 3½" square of black wool for scalloped border
- ✕ 2 squares, 5" × 5", of lightweight fusible interfacing
- ✕ Pearl cotton, size 12, in black and gold
- ✕ Fiberfill stuffing

*The bowl filler shown is made from On Point cotton by Maywood Studio.

Stitching and Assembly

1 Fuse the interfacing to the wrong sides of the cream cotton and gold wool squares, following the manufacturer's instructions.

2 Use the pattern below to cut the scalloped border from the black wool.

3 Position and pin the border on the cream square and whipstitch it in place using black pearl cotton.

4 Use gold pearl cotton to sew a French knot in each scallop.

5 Transfer the words *Be Happy* from the pattern onto the cream cotton and backstitch them using black pearl cotton.

6 Trim the stitched piece to 4" square, keeping the design centered.

7 Referring to "Assembling the Bowl Fillers" (page 11), sew and stuff the pillow.

> Appliqué patterns do not include seam allowances.

Border
Cut 1 black.

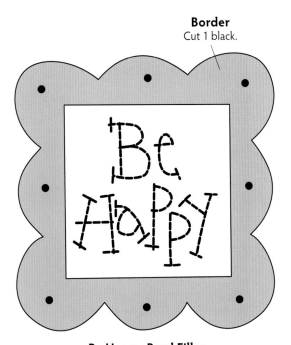

Be Happy Bowl Filler

Embroidery Key

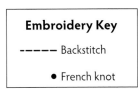

- - - - - Backstitch

● French knot

Floral Be Brave

Materials

- × 6½" × 6½" square of gray cotton for front*
- × 6½" × 6½" square of cream polka-dot cotton for back
- × 5" × 5" square of black wool for scalloped border
- × 2 squares, 6½" × 6½", of lightweight fusible interfacing
- × Pearl cotton, size 12, in black, green, white, and gold
- × Fiberfill stuffing

*The bowl filler shown is made from Daiwabo Taupe Woven.

Stitching and Assembly

1 Fuse the interfacing to the wrong sides of the gray and cream polka-dot squares, following the manufacturer's instructions.

2 Use the pattern below to cut the scalloped border from the black wool square.

3 Position and pin the scalloped border on the gray cotton and whipstitch it in place with black pearl cotton.

4 Use gold pearl cotton to sew a running stitch parallel to the inner edge of the scalloped border.

5 Transfer the embroidery designs from the pattern to the center of the appliquéd front.

6 Backstitch the words *be brave* using black pearl cotton.

7 Sew the flower with white pearl cotton and a lazy daisy stitch. Make a French knot in the center of the flower with gold pearl cotton.

8 Stitch the vines and leaves with a backstitch and green pearl cotton. Make a French knot with white pearl cotton at the base of each pair of leaves.

9 Trim the stitched piece to 5½" square.

10 Referring to "Assembling the Bowl Fillers" (page 11), sew and stuff the pillow.

Appliqué patterns do not include seam allowances.

Border
Cut 1 black.

Floral Be Brave Bowl Filler

Embroidery Key

----- Backstitch

● French knot

⬭ Lazy daisy

– – – Running stitch

Be Strong and Bloom

FINISHED SIZE
5½" × 6½"

Materials

- × 7" × 8" rectangle of cream polka-dot cotton for front
- × 7" × 8" rectangle of plaid cotton for back
- × 4" × 4" square of gold textured wool for bee skep
- × 2" × 7" rectangle of green wool for stem, grass, and leaves
- × 2" × 3" rectangle of white wool for daisy petals
- × 1½" × 1½" square of yellow wool for daisy center and bee
- × 1" × 1½" rectangle of black wool for bee skep door
- × 2 rectangles, 7" × 8", of lightweight fusible interfacing
- × Pearl cotton, size 12, in black, gold, green, and white
- × Black cotton quilting thread
- × Fiberfill stuffing

Stitching and Assembly

1 Fuse the interfacing to the wrong sides of the polka-dot and plaid rectangles, following the manufacturer's instructions.

2 Use the patterns (page 57) to cut the bee skep, bee, door, grass, stem, leaves, daisy petals, and daisy center from the wool pieces.

3 Position and pin the appliqué pieces on the polka-dot cotton.

4 Use gold pearl cotton to blanket-stitch the bee skep and add backstitches to create horizontal lines as shown on the pattern.

5 Whipstitch the grass, stem, and leaves with green pearl cotton. Add lazy daisy stitches to the centers of the leaves.

6 Whipstitch the daisy center with gold pearl cotton and whipstitch the daisy petals with white pearl cotton.

7 Whipstitch the door with black pearl cotton.

8 Whipstitch the bee with gold pearl cotton. Use white pearl cotton to sew lazy daisy stitches for the bee's wings. Sew straight stitches across the bee's body with black quilting thread to create the stripes.

9 Trim the stitched piece to 6" × 7".

10 Referring to "Assembling the Bowl Fillers" (page 11), sew and stuff the pillow.

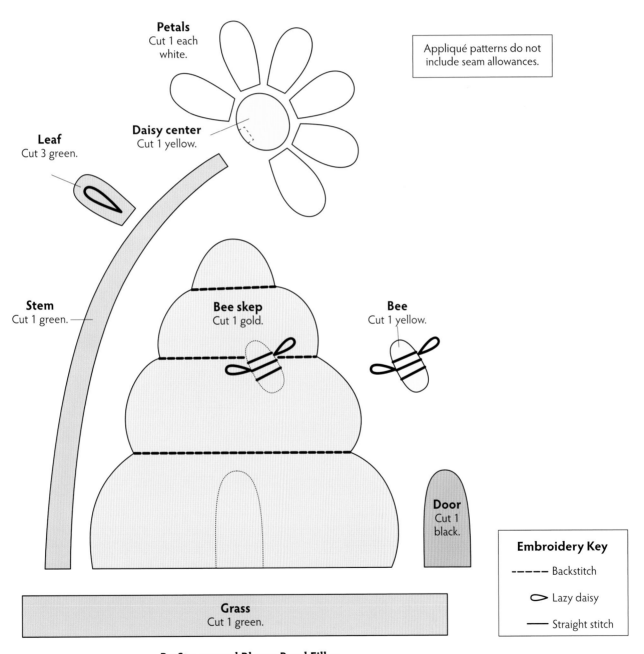

Petals
Cut 1 each white.

Leaf
Cut 3 green.

Daisy center
Cut 1 yellow.

Appliqué patterns do not include seam allowances.

Stem
Cut 1 green.

Bee skep
Cut 1 gold.

Bee
Cut 1 yellow.

Door
Cut 1 black.

Embroidery Key

- - - - - Backstitch

⌒ Lazy daisy

—— Straight stitch

Grass
Cut 1 green.

Be Strong and Bloom Bowl Filler

Be Sweet Daisy

Materials

- ✕ 6" × 6" square of gray cotton for front*
- ✕ 6" × 6" square of gold wool for back
- ✕ 5" × 5" square of white wool for daisy
- ✕ 2" × 2" square of dark gold wool for large daisy center
- ✕ 1½" × 1½" square of light gold wool for small daisy center
- ✕ 2 squares, 6" × 6", of lightweight fusible interfacing
- ✕ Pearl cotton, size 12, in cream, gold, and white
- ✕ 1 gold button, ½" diameter, for daisy center
- ✕ Fiberfill stuffing

The bowl filler shown is made from Daiwabo Taupe Woven.

Stitching and Assembly

1 Fuse the interfacing to the wrong sides of the gray cotton and gold wool squares, following the manufacturer's instructions.

2 Use the patterns below to cut the appliqué pieces from the wool as directed.

3 Position and pin the appliqué pieces in the center of the gray cotton. Blanket-stitch them in place with coordinating pearl cotton.

4 Use white pearl cotton to backstitch around each flower petal inside the blanket stitch.

5 Use cream pearl cotton to sew straight stitches with couching through the center of each petal.

6 Trim the stitched piece to 5" square.

7 Referring to "Assembling the Bowl Fillers" (page 11), sew and stuff the pillow.

8 Sew the button to the center of the flower, stitching through the back of the bowl filler to create a slight indentation in the center.

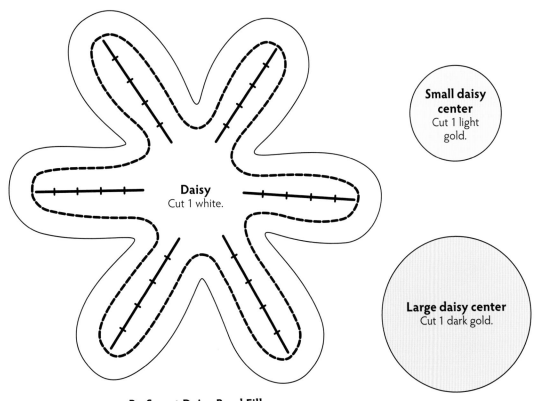

Appliqué patterns do not include seam allowances.

Daisy
Cut 1 white.

Small daisy center
Cut 1 light gold.

Large daisy center
Cut 1 dark gold.

Be Sweet Daisy Bowl Filler

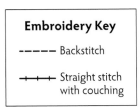

Embroidery Key

- - - - - Backstitch

+ + + + + Straight stitch with couching

chalk talk

It's hard to find a chalkboard in schools these days, but decorating with them is all the rage! You can add cute bowls of chalkboard decor to any room with some black fabric, a little embroidery, and a bit of chalk dust.

Gather in Love

FINISHED SIZE
5" DIAMETER

Materials

- ✕ 7" × 7" square of black cotton for front
- ✕ 7" × 7" square of black-and-white striped cotton for back
- ✕ 2 squares, 7" × 7", of lightweight fusible interfacing
- ✕ White pearl cotton, size 12
- ✕ White quilting thread
- ✕ 18" length of ½"-wide black cotton rickrack
- ✕ White Uni-ball Signo Broad gel pen
- ✕ Fiberfill stuffing
- ✕ White chalk

Stitching and Assembly

1 Fuse the interfacing to the wrong sides of the black and striped squares, following the manufacturer's instructions.

2 Transfer all embroidery lines and letters from the pattern (page 62) onto the black cotton. Also trace the outer circle, which will be the cutting line after stitching.

3 Backstitch the word *gather*, the heart, and lines in the heart using white pearl cotton.

4 Backstitch the words *in love* using white quilting thread. Add a French knot above the *i*.

5 Stem-stitch the vine with white pearl cotton and make lazy daisy stitches for the leaves.

6 Use the gel pen to color the letters *g*, *a*, *h*, and *e* as shown in the photo on page 61 to add highlights. Color the centers of the leaves and the heart and let dry.

7 Trim the stitched piece, cutting the circle along the outer traced line.

8 Referring to "Assembling the Bowl Fillers" (page 11), sew and stuff the pillow.

9 Pin the rickrack around the seamline of the bowl filler and hand stitch in place.

10 Rub the side of a piece of white chalk back and forth over the bowl filler front to give it a chalkboard look.

Embroidery Key	
- - - - -	Backstitch
●	French knot
⌒	Lazy daisy
⟋⟍⟋⟍	Stem stitch

Gather in Love Bowl Filler

Welcome Home

FINISHED SIZE
5¾" × 3"

Materials

- × 4" × 7" rectangle of black cotton for front
- × 4" × 7" rectangle of black-and-gray plaid cotton for back
- × 2 rectangles, 4" × 7", of lightweight fusible interfacing
- × White pearl cotton, size 12
- × White quilting thread
- × 4 buttons, ⅜" diameter
- × Fiberfill stuffing
- × White chalk

Stitching and Assembly

1 Fuse the interfacing to the wrong sides of the black and plaid rectangles, following the manufacturer's instructions.

2 Transfer all embroidery lines and letters from the pattern (page 64) onto the black cotton.

3 Use the white pearl cotton to backstitch the word *welcome* and the scallops and also to stitch French knots above the scallops.

4 Backstitch the word *home* using white quilting thread.

5 Sew the four buttons in place below the scallops.

6 Trim the stitched piece to 6¼" × 3½ ", keeping the design centered.

7 Referring to "Assembling the Bowl Fillers" (page 11), sew and stuff the pillow.

8 Rub the side of a piece of white chalk back and forth over the bowl filler front to give it a chalkboard look.

Button placement →

Welcome Home Bowl Filler

Embroidery Key
- - - - - Backstitch
● French knot

Have Courage and Be Kind

FINISHED SIZE
7" × 3"

Materials

- ✗ 3½" × 9" rectangle of black cotton for front
- ✗ 2" × 9" rectangle of black-and-white striped cotton for front
- ✗ 5" × 9" rectangle of black-and-gray plaid cotton for back
- ✗ 2 rectangles, 5" × 9", of lightweight fusible interfacing
- ✗ White quilting thread
- ✗ 12 assorted white and cream buttons, ⅜" diameter
- ✗ Black thread for buttons
- ✗ Fiberfill stuffing
- ✗ White chalk

Stitching and Assembly

Press the seam allowances as shown by the arrow.

1 Sew the stripe 2" × 9" rectangle to the black 3½" × 9" rectangle to create the front, which should measure 5" × 9", including seam allowances.

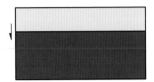

Make 1 unit,
5" × 9".

2 Fuse the interfacing to the wrong sides of the pieced front and plaid rectangle, following the manufacturer's instructions.

3 Transfer all embroidery lines and letters from the pattern below onto the black section of the front.

4 Backstitch the words *have courage & be kind* and the underline using white quilting thread. Dot the *i* with a French knot.

5 Sew the 12 buttons in place below the underline using black thread.

6 Trim the stitched piece to measure 7½" × 3½".

7 Referring to "Assembling the Bowl Fillers" (page 11), sew and stuff the pillow.

8 Rub the side of a piece of white chalk back and forth over the bowl filler front to give it a chalkboard look.

Button placement

Have Courage and Be Kind Bowl Filler

Embroidery Key
- - - - - Backstitch
● French knot

Chalkboard Be Brave

Materials

* ✗ 5½" × 5½" square of black cotton for front
* ✗ 5½" × 5½" square of black-and-white plaid cotton for back
* ✗ 2 squares, 5½" × 5½", of lightweight fusible interfacing
* ✗ White quilting thread
* ✗ White pearl cotton, size 12
* ✗ White Uni-ball Signo Broad gel pen
* ✗ Fiberfill stuffing
* ✗ White chalk

Stitching and Assembly

1 Fuse the interfacing to the wrong sides of the black and plaid squares, following the manufacturer's instructions.

2 Transfer all embroidery lines and *be brave* from the pattern below onto the black cotton. Also trace the solid circle outline, which will be the cutting line after the stitching is complete.

3 Backstitch the words *be brave* and the wreath using white quilting thread.

4 Using white pearl cotton, make lazy daisy stitches for the leaves and sew a French knot in the center of each pair of leaves.

5 Color the open spaces in the center of the leaves with the gel pen and let dry.

6 Cut the circle from the stitched piece following the outer traced line.

7 Referring to "Assembling the Bowl Fillers" (page 11), sew and stuff the pillow.

8 Rub the side of a piece of white chalk back and forth over the bowl filler front to give it a chalkboard look.

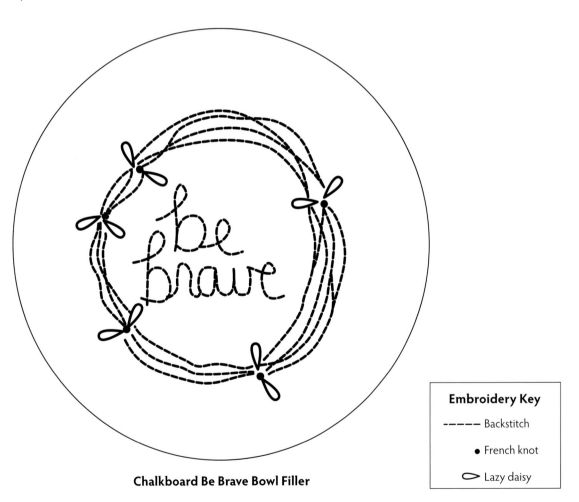

Chalkboard Be Brave Bowl Filler

Embroidery Key

- - - - - Backstitch

● French knot

⌒ Lazy daisy

Love Banner

FINISHED SIZE
5" × 2½"

Materials

× 4" × 6" rectangle of black cotton for front

× 4" × 6" rectangle of black-and-white plaid cotton for back

× 2 rectangles, 4" × 6", of lightweight fusible interfacing

× White pearl cotton, size 12

× White Uni-ball Signo Broad gel pen

× Fiberfill stuffing

× White chalk

Stitching and Assembly

1 Fuse the interfacing to the wrong sides of the black and plaid rectangles, following the manufacturer's instructions.

2 Transfer all embroidery lines and the word *love* from the pattern (page 70) onto the black cotton.

3 Using white pearl cotton, stitch the banner cord with a stem stitch.

6 Color the inside areas of the pennants with the gel pen and let dry.

7 Trim the stitched piece to 5½" × 3", keeping the design centered.

8 Referring to "Assembling the Bowl Fillers" (page 11), sew and stuff the pillow.

9 Rub the side of a piece of white chalk back and forth over the bowl filler to give it a chalkboard look.

4 Backstitch the pennants and the letters *L, o, v,* and *e* using white pearl cotton.

5 Using white pearl cotton, make the bows with a lazy daisy stitch and the backstitch, and add a French knot in the center of each bow.

Love Banner Bowl Filler

Embroidery Key

- - - - Backstitch

● French knot

◯ Lazy daisy

〜 Stem stitch

cabin in the woods

I wish I may, I wish I might, have the wish I wish tonight. Get cozy by the fire late at night and relax while stitching up these charming woodsy bowl fillers.

Nighttime Forest

FINISHED SIZE
5½" × 4½"

Materials

- ✖ 6" × 7" rectangle of black wool for front
- ✖ 6" × 7" rectangle of cotton flannel for back
- ✖ 4" × 7" rectangle of green wool for trees and grass
- ✖ 3" × 3" square of brown wool for tree trunks
- ✖ 2 rectangles, 6" × 7", of lightweight fusible interfacing
- ✖ Pearl cotton, size 12, in brown and green
- ✖ Fiberfill stuffing

Stitching and Assembly

1 Fuse the interfacing to the wrong sides of the black wool and flannel rectangles, following the manufacturer's instructions.

2 Use the patterns (page 73) to cut the appliqué pieces from the green and brown wool.

3 Align the green wool grass piece with the bottom edge of the black wool and center it from side to side. The bottom edge of the green wool will be sewn into the seam allowance later.

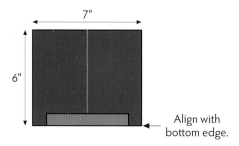

7"

6"

Align with bottom edge.

4 Position and pin the appliqué pieces on the black wool. Whipstitch them in place with coordinating pearl cotton.

5 Use green pearl cotton to sew straight stitches inside the green trees as decorative stitching.

6 Use brown pearl cotton to add cross-stitches to the tree trunks.

7 Trim the stitched piece to 6" × 5", measuring from the bottom and keeping the design centered from left to right.

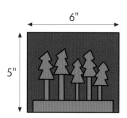

6"

5"

Trimming guide

8 Referring to "Assembling the Bowl Fillers" (page 11), sew and stuff the pillow.

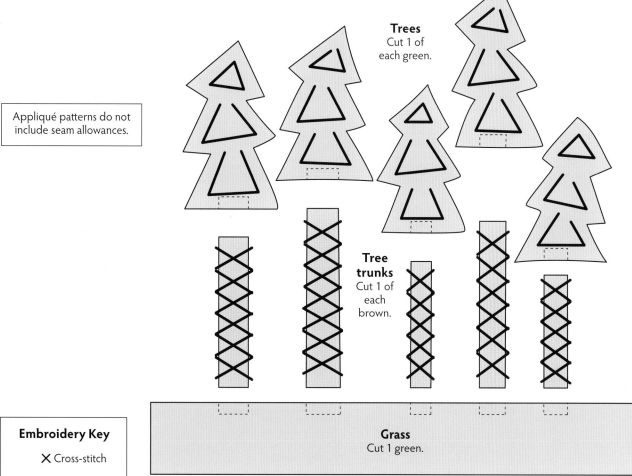

Appliqué patterns do not include seam allowances.

Trees
Cut 1 of each green.

Tree trunks
Cut 1 of each brown.

Grass
Cut 1 green.

Embroidery Key

X Cross-stitch

— Straight stitch

Nighttime Forest Bowl Filler

Little Cabin
in the Woods

FINISHED SIZE
4½" × 5"

Materials

- ✗ 6" × 6½" rectangle of black wool for front
- ✗ 6" × 6½" rectangle of dark cotton for back
- ✗ 2½" × 2½" square of cream wool for cabin
- ✗ 2" × 3" rectangle of brown wool for door and roof
- ✗ 1½" × 3½" rectangle of brown tweed wool for chimney
- ✗ 1" × 2" rectangle of gold wool for moon
- ✗ 2 rectangles, 6" × 6½", of lightweight fusible interfacing
- ✗ Pearl cotton, size 12, in cream, brown, dark brown, and gold
- ✗ Gold cotton quilting thread
- ✗ Fiberfill stuffing

Stitching and Assembly

1 Fuse the interfacing to the wrong sides of the black wool and dark cotton rectangles, following the manufacturer's instructions.

2 Use the patterns below to cut the cabin, door, roof, chimney, and moon from the wool pieces.

3 Position and pin the cabin, roof, and chimney on the black wool. Whipstitch in place with coordinating pearl cotton.

4 Use a double strand of the dark brown pearl cotton to sew long straight stitches across the cabin. Add couching stitches to tack the thread in place.

5 Position and pin the door in place and whipstitch with brown pearl cotton.

6 Position and pin the moon above the cabin and whipstitch with gold pearl cotton.

7 Make little stars using straight stitches and a single strand of gold quilting thread.

8 Trim the piece to 5" × 5½", keeping the design centered.

9 Referring to "Assembling the Bowl Fillers" (page 11), sew and stuff the pillow.

> Appliqué patterns do not include seam allowances.

Moon
Cut 1 gold.

Roof
Cut 1 brown.

Cabin
Cut 1 cream.

Chimney
Cut 1 brown tweed.

Door
Cut 1 brown.

Little Cabin in the Woods Bowl Filler

Embroidery Key

— Straight stitch

+++++ Straight stitch with couching

Relax

Materials

- ✗ 5" × 6" rectangle of black wool for front
- ✗ 5" × 6" rectangle of dark cotton for back
- ✗ 3" × 3" square of gold wool for star
- ✗ 2 rectangles, 5" × 6", of lightweight fusible interfacing
- ✗ Pearl cotton, size 12, in gold and cream
- ✗ Fiberfill stuffing

Stitching and Assembly

1 Fuse the interfacing to the wrong sides of the black wool and dark cotton rectangles, following the manufacturer's instructions.

2 Use the pattern below to cut the star from gold wool.

3 Position and pin the star on the black wool and blanket-stitch with gold pearl cotton.

4 Use gold pearl cotton to make straight stitches on the star from one point to the other. Add couching stitches to hold the thread in place.

5 Transfer the word *relax* from the pattern onto the background. Backstitch using cream pearl cotton.

6 Use gold pearl cotton to add several small stars with straight stitches.

7 Trim the stitched piece to 5" × 4".

8 Referring to "Assembling the Bowl Fillers" (page 11), sew and stuff the pillow.

> Appliqué patterns do not include seam allowances.

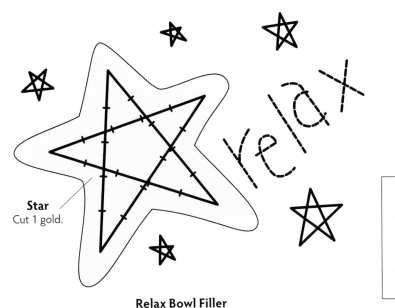

Star
Cut 1 gold.

Relax Bowl Filler

Embroidery Key

----- Backstitch

—— Straight stitch

++++ Straight stitch with couching

Wish upon a Star

FINISHED SIZE
5¼" × 5¼"
(approximately)

Materials

✗ 2 squares, 7" × 7", of gold (print or solid) cotton for front and back

✗ 1¼" × 2¼" rectangle of white cotton for front

✗ Gray quilting thread

✗ Gray permanent fabric marker (optional)

✗ Template plastic or cardstock

✗ Fiberfill stuffing

✗ 1 yard of black ⅛"-wide ribbon

✗ Large-eye needle for ribbon (optional)

Stitching and Assembly

<u>1</u> Use the star pattern (page 79) to make a template.

<u>2</u> Place the template on the wrong side of one of the gold squares and trace around it. Do not cut out the star.

<u>3</u> Layer the two gold squares right sides together, aligning the raw edges. Pin at the corners to keep the layers from shifting.

4 Sew on the traced line all the way around. Trim the excess fabric ¼" from the stitching line.

5 Carefully cut a 1½" slit through one side to create an opening for turning and stuffing. Clip the inside corners and trim the points, making sure not to cut into the stitching.

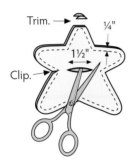

Trim. →
¼"
1½"
Clip. →

6 Turn right side out and stuff.

7 Whipstitch the opening closed.

8 Transfer the word *wish* from the pattern to the white cotton rectangle. Backstitch using gray quilting thread. Or use a gray marker to simply draw the letters. Cover the opening with the rectangle and whipstitch it in place.

9 Add a ribbon hanger using a large-eye needle or attach the ribbon to the top of the star with a few tack stitches.

Wish

Embroidery Key

- - - - - Backstitch

● French knot

Star

Wish upon a Star Bowl Filler

Acknowledgments

A never-ending thank-you to my best friend and husband, Jeff, who bought me my first sewing machine, has always believed in me, and helps me believe in myself.

Thank you to the very special team at Martingale for inviting me on this journey to share my love of hand stitching with so many others.

Resources

WOOL FABRIC

Heavens to Betsy
Heavens-to-Betsy.com

Marcus Fabrics
MarcusFabrics.com
I used some of their wool and aged muslin, and they have a great black basecloth that would work well for these projects also.

Weeks Dye Works
WeeksDyeWorks.com

SPECIALTY THREADS

Rustic Wool Moire
Pinwheels.com

Valdani
Valdani.com
Check the website for distributors in your area.

DOILY HEARTS

Factory Direct Craft
FactoryDirectCraft.com
3" ivory heart doily

TEXTURED COTTON FABRIC

Daiwabo Japanese Woven
Daiwabo.co.jp
Check the website for distributors in your area.

Diamond Textiles
DiamondTextilesUSA.com
Check the website for distributors in your area.

ABOUT THE AUTHOR

Debbie grew up in the Pacific Northwest with her three sisters, moving every summer between Oregon and Washington for their father's job. They had many matching dresses made by their mother, and thanks to their grandmother, a never-ending supply of Barbie doll clothes.

It was those things handmade by her mother and grandmother that inspired Debbie to fall in love with needle and thread. After finally settling in the Portland area in her high school years, she continued to learn to sew in home economics class. After she met and married her husband, Jeff, their first joint purchase was a Kenmore sewing machine from Sears, Roebuck and Co. During the first 10 years of their marriage, Debbie sewed many of her own clothes to save money, and she eventually moved on to sewing clothes for her children, other family members, and friends. After her children were past the age when they would wear homemade clothes, Debbie and her mother sewed and sold items in craft fairs. Her mother was a great source of encouragement, and toward the end of her struggle with cancer, she encouraged Debbie to try designing original patterns. Before her mother passed away in 2001, Debbie promised that she would give it a try. Debbie has now been designing since 2002.

When she is not stitching and designing for her business, Wooden Spool Designs, Debbie loves to work in the garden, walk on the beach, and spend time with her grandchildren. With her recently retired husband, Debbie is off on new adventures and moving to Idaho.